shades
of gold

allie wisniewski

First printing: 2017

ISBN-13: 978-0692974087
ISBN-10: 0692974083

"Logic only gives man what he needs. Magic gives him what he wants."

– *Tom Robbins*

A Fable

Says Self to the Ego,

"Have you had enough of yourself quite yet?"

Says Ego to the Self,

"Perhaps tomorrow I'll be satisfied."

April

There's no inkling of the past
In the sweetness on my tongue.
I ease the grief of shattered self
With flowers, tea, and sun.
The echoes of resounding spring
Will coax a heaving lung,
But severed hearts of winters gone
By April will be numb.
I bask in speckled starlight and
I weep with leaking skies.
The endless rains of warmer days
Are tonics in disguise.

Sincerity

Messy lover,

Candid lover,

Lie down with me here.

Sip pretty nonsense from my dainty teacup and then

Shatter it on the floor.

I speak nothing pleasant of pleasantries.

Spit shards of empty mutterings into my hands,

And I'll toss them

Out the window.

Only Rarely is Silence Transparent

Spirit stretched by watercolored mornings

And evenings rose golden,

Swelling heart and lungs alike

Breathe the clarity of silence.

Shade my skin with tones of earth,

Dust my soles with rusty pigments.

The wind braids wildness into my hair

And mists my glistening body.

Soul drenched in life's elixirs:

Water, sunshine, sweat;

I tremble at the feet of the Mother,

Bowing deeply to her untamed glory.

Lovers' Lament

I will stain your carpet with my love;

The breeze cannot carry my scent

Away.

You cannot wring me out,

Slip me out the back door,

Pry my grip from your memory.

Your breakfast will always taste

Like me.

I will finger-paint your walls with my love,

And every morning,

You will remember.

Rotting

He eyes my vibrant skin and

Sniffs the air around me,

Saturated with the aroma of

Neglect.

His gaze is charged no longer with

Lusty hunger but with

Disappointed

Concession.

I was beautiful and ripe when he

Plucked me from the tree,

Aching for a treat or

Just a taste of

Something sweet.

So gently he set me on the window sill,

Intent on saving me

For later.

But now I think that later

Will never come.

Because later is much too late,

And too long to wait,

For not everything that is beautiful

Is forever.

Death is Beautiful

The earth, it claims my body and

Collects me in its arms.

No need for me to fight or thrash,

By death it means no harm.

My soul too heavy for the ride,

It bids my shell good day,

And spreads like seed in fields of grass:

New life born from decay.

Perhaps I fear uncertain fate,

But in my final hours,

My comfort lies in knowing

Soon,

I'll join the wildflowers.

OH, TO BE ALIVE

THERE IS NO VOID AND YOU ARE
NOT SHOUTING INTO IT.

EVERY INCH OF SPACE IS INHABITED
FULLY AND COMPLETELY.

SPIRIT MAKES A HOME
IN EVERY CORNER.

WE KEEP OURSELVES COMPANY
WITH OUR MANY PERSONALITIES.

AND OUR BODIES DANCE
TO THE TUNE OF DIVINITY.

WE ARE NOT AFRAID.
WE ARE AWAKE AND

ALIVE.

Morning Moon

Oh Luna,

I wish to taste your sweet cosmic flesh,

To take a bite out of you,

Run my tongue over your rocky craters,

Savor the crunch of your solar reflection,

Swallow you whole and

Still the ocean tides.

Disarray

Mindful writing,

Scribbling,

Scrawling.

Feeling the smooth flow of ink

As it decorates the paper,

Stealing without remorse its

Porcelain virginity.

If I must tread lightly on the Earth,

I will find a place to

Stomp and

Roll around.

I want to

Make a mess and

Not have to clean it up.

I need somewhere I can

Dump things out and

Leave them there.

I kiss the pages,

Grateful for

My beautiful

Disarray.

Dandelion

A wispy tuft of dandelion

Floats by my lowered gaze,

Quite easily the softest speck

Of life I've seen today.

"So, how far have you traveled?

Traversed you land and sea?

Where began the gust of wind

that brought you here to me?"

This overarching question,

One I ponder as we speak,

Is the question which I long to pose

To everyone I meet.

Mindscapes

I appreciate substance

So deeply.

I want to watch you

Ignite as you speak,

Stoke your soul flame with

My conscious attention to

Your passionate spilling.

Inspire me with stories untold,

Words unfolding,

Cascading showers of

Decorated time.

Materialize your thoughts and

Let me drink them in.

Let's explore our mindscapes

Together.

This is the ultimate

Adventure.

Prana

I whisper

To the Earth mother,

"Can you hear

My breathing?

Because,

I can surely

hear yours."

As a Cape

I am almost completely shattered.

I am jagged fragments suspended in

A beam of light, I am

Frazzled and moving

Too quickly downstream, it is all

Rushing past

Far too quickly, I can hardly

Make sense of any of it, but

Nothing feels bad I am just

Steeping

In the present

Always

In the present, I can't even

Write prose anymore, it is all

Poetry.

I am so alive that

The roses stop to smell me, I am

Electric and

I know that there is no absence of

Time, but still every morning I wake up

Exhausted.

I've found this virtue to be slowly

Hollowing and

Righteous clarity to drape over me a transparency I

Cannot afford.

And so I wear my vices

As a cape

Or on those next mornings as a

Blanket, sheltering this cage of flesh which has long since

Turned to glass,

Etching promises of doomsday into my hardened

exterior in

Cryptic tongues.

Do you think I could have saved

That fearless fairy child,

Standing four-feet-ten in

One sock and

Bathed in blissful naivety?

With fragility dead and gone the wind has thrown

Caution back to me, now, and

I know that I am

Nine birthdays too late.

Reflecting here I see that

Blowing out a candle on a cake I

Never asked for, that's

More than a gust of breath and

Spit and

Smoke-laden frosting, that's

Another year of playing the game and

Never winning, of

Crude desensitization, of

Am I doing this right? Of

A thousand answers that aren't mine and

Another row of empty bottles

On the shelf.

Dragon Girl

I am a

Fire-breathing dragon and

I will be slain by

No man.

No knight in shining armor

Will ever extinguish

My flame.

Self and I

There is no question that I am

More than my mind.

Only a sliver of my being

Resides within this earthly vessel.

And yet,

There is no emptiness.

I am graced always with the presence

Of Self.

With Self I fill every vacant cavity

In my earthly body.

A joyful light

Fills me to the brim —

Every love I've ever known

Runs through me

Like glitter glue in my veins.

This is all perfectly instrumented;

I am at home

In my own company.

Self and I,

We walk together through the grass,

And discuss

Our favorite shades of green.

Untouchable

So often I find myself

Alone

Opening wide

The legs of my mind

For beautiful men

Strangers

And closing them

Tightly again

When they come too close

With their pokers and

Probes

Seeking to lobotomize

A heart so soft and

Unfamiliar

That they'd fear for the fate

Of their hands

Should they feel so emboldened

To touch it

Rebirth

Spring, you beautiful awakening

Post-coma's first breath

White death resurrection

May

Who painted the grass with

Begonias and

Wild roses?

Spring,

A thoughtful vandal,

Leaving its mark in the way that it does

So ephemerally

For our temporary admiration,

Our momentary bliss,

And vanishing again

As quickly

As it comes,

Stealing away the dimensional vibrancy

Which we press in our books

And photograph

To sustain ourselves

As we endure the world's three season long

Exhalation.

Summer in the City

The air drips with the scent of

Fresh cut grass and

I am transported

To my childhood,

Drowning in my own sweat,

Both body and mind

Suffocated

By a Florida July.

My shirt sticks to my skin and

My skin sticks to my bones

As if hanging on

For dear life.

My body, mimicking my mind,

Engulfed in a summer flame and

Terrified

To melt away.

Everything is Possible

Unzip yourself and step outside

Into the evening sun.

The breeze smells like

A rainbow and

The flowers taste like

Rum.

Walk gracefully through fields and streams,

As if the world were glass.

It is because it can be, so

What more is there

To ask?

I Am Not a Cactus

I know I can be prickly, but

Please do not compare me

To a cactus.

You cannot sprinkle me with water

Every few months or so and

Expect me to be fine.

I will not flourish on the window sill,

Immune to the wrath of the sun.

I cannot stash what little you have given me

For a later date,

When perhaps I'll need it more.

There is no tomorrow without

Love today, because

I have mostly drained

My reservoir.

Shadow Work

Interdimensional,

Beaming up and

Free falling back down,

Learning and forgetting and

Learning again,

Remembering this time,

Tumbling into the abyss,

Finding it to be more comfortable

Than expected.

Making peace

With the darkness.

Emptying muddy water in

The pond of my mind,

Bucket by bucket,

Until the eternal spring within me

Has refilled it and it is

Still

And

Clear.

Death Wish

I breathe you in

Inhale your essence as you speak

Your words, your energy

Intoxicate me

And simultaneously

Blacken my lungs

This toxic smoke

Will surely kill me

But I cannot bring myself

To exhale

Florida Feet

I always told you I had

Florida feet,

Invincible and

Oblivious to the heat and

The grit of the

Concrete.

The summer sand has

Seared them proper and

Long since gifted me its

Final blisters.

Calloused, weathered,

Sliced by the stealth of

Hidden oyster beds and then

Immortalized in the elixir of

The sea.

So, no, I will not

Wear shoes today.

These Florida feet have

Walked a thousand barefoot miles

Through the pines and the swamp lands,

And still carried me home in time

For dinner.

Four Things You Don't Get to Decide for Me

What is hard

What is easy

What is beautiful

What is worth it

Born of Green

Concrete and I are like

Oil and water.

You can contain us here

In the same jar,

But we will never

Mix.

Return me to the

Land of green, where

I am strangled by the

Jasmine and not

Cigarette smoke on a

Smoggy afternoon.

I cannot wrestle with steel

Any longer, because

It always wins and

I'd rather lose to

The Mother than

The Man.

There's a Human in There

We pass building after building

And never wonder

What's inside.

We pass body after body

And never wonder

What's inside.

A Cosmic Symphony

I hear the music in the leaves,

I hear it in the waves.

I hear the song of every book

Each time I turn a page.

I hear the music in the trees,

I hear it in the birds.

I hear the beat in hearts and brains

And syllables of words.

I hear the music in the rain,

In winds through desert sands.

And to this cosmic symphony,

I leap

And twirl

And dance.

Soul Shell

I am only Self,

And so little of me

Is this soul shell.

Physicality is futile.

My hair cannot tell you

How many lives

I have lived.

This body is simply

Ephemeral, and

Mirrors are hardly

Reassuring.

Chi

When I am alone

With the trees,

I am alone

With myself.

Quiet

I sit in quiet stillness,

Stained with morning's remnants,

As God whispers through the leaves.

I speak to the Muse,

And she answers me

With birdsong.

My spirit dances,

And in the air there is

No perfume of tomorrow.

Leaving the Nest

At the breakfast table —
Visions of my mother
Slicing strawberries
For my cereal.

Her hands:
Purposeful, skilled.
Beholding a lifetime
Of textured dexterity.

And now I sit,
Alone in the same chair,
Stirring milk
Into my coffee.

No longer bound here
By dependence,
I slice strawberries
For my cereal.

Depth

Yes, I often sit and think about all the times

I was wrong.

And I wonder if you think about them as often

As I do.

It seems that I make mountains

Out of molehills.

All my lovers have told me

Silently.

I fear that I feel everything so deeply

That I can hardly make the distinction

Between them.

Most Everything is Gray

All too quickly, the good enough

Was gone,

And the only adequacy we fostered

Was in the way we conversed

With our tongues.

Time after time,

Words failed to consecrate

Our understanding,

Left to dangle pathetically in the empty space

Where love should have been.

And so without fail,

The inky blackness of night returned

To overtake me.

I felt my way through the void,

Tripping over our skeletal remains,

Longing for the warm embrace of the familiar.

For hours,

I sat on the front steps of the morning,

Waiting for it to let me in.

I'd come to find that it was hardly ever lonely

In the place between the darkness

and the light.

Untitled

He was selfish

Even in his generosity,

Giving only what he could afford

To lose.

Everything is Temporary

I'm sorry but

I have to take this —

The day is calling and

I cannot stay long.

Did you hear that

This life is temporary? Fleeting?

I heard it through the grapevine and

I know that I can no longer

Waste another second

Without the sun

On my skin.

The moon is rising and

I only wish now that

I had said what I wanted to say

When I wanted

To say it.

Soil-Bound Beings

With trunks

Oak-strong —

Rooted,

Reaching.

In the Arms of the Morning

And now I can't stop dreaming

Of an eternal sunrise —

One where I sit and stare in awe,

As God smears her colors

Across the sky.

Fluid and variable,

An everlasting display,

Forever and ever.

Find me in the arms

Of the morning.

Gentleness

I watched him slide his hands around her waist,

Kissing her shoulder softly

With a kind of gentleness that I had seen in him

Only twice:

When he was asleep, and

When he was in love.

In My Veins

There are days I wish the rain would stop
And days that I pretend
That drenched under a weeping sky
The rain would never end.
An endless, steady shower,
Flooding fields and streets and brains,
Sopping wet, my pruning skin
Forever water-stained.
"Cleanse my conscience, make me whole,"
I whisper to the clouds.
Lightning often crashes, but
My thoughts are just as loud.
And wading through the rising tides,
I realize what I've done.
Drowning in the misty gray,
I long to feel the sun.
I know that soon the rain will stop,
For so much time has passed.
Soaked to the bone with trembling hands,
I'll see the light at last.
A golden glow will dry the earth,
Few puddles will remain.
But the storm within me rages on —
The rain is in my veins.

I Am Only You

You're my favorite scent,

My favorite sound,

My favorite sight and hue.

You've no trouble understanding me,

'Cause all of me

Is you.

Unbound

Dwellers in body know

Only of the tangible.

How lonely it must be to

Exist solely in the

Physical plane.

Dwellers in spirit…

Now, they know of the magic.

The ethereal glow

Of being that is Source —

The divine which

Paints the sky and

Combs the hair of tangled

Grasslands and

Cues the choir of sparrows

In the morning.

Power Trip

How you love it when I need you,

How I fuel your wretched fire,

You stand, amused, in silence

As I smolder on the pyre.

Do you snicker on your self-made throne

As I whimper at your feet?

When I sing my desperate longings,

Do you whistle to the beat?

You adore when I beseech you,

For your reign is thus affirmed.

No longer can I stand to beg,

Your love I will not earn.

I've no more time to wait for you,

Our season's due to pass,

I'll gladly get the door, my dear;

Don't let it hit your ass.

Stop Calling Me Pretty

"You're so pretty," he said,
But I caught the silence in the wake of those
Three little words
Which look so nice on paper,
"Pretty,"
A fragment of a gesture, which
Should mean something to somebody, but
Now means nothing
To me.
"Pretty,"
Because any more than that
Would handcuff him; He says,
"Don't touch my wrists,
But let me touch yours,
Let me grab them and
Hold them so tightly you'd
Mistake my grip for some
Half-passionate embrace,
Don't struggle,
This is enough for you,
I am enough for you,
I am all that you deserve,
And pretty is all that
You are."

He Told Me My Voice Was Like Chamomile Tea

Words brewed for you

Steep

Beneath my tongue and

Spill like

Chamomile tea.

So sickly saccharine,

You're quick

To swallow soft sedation.

Apothecary girl, I am,

With all my herbal

Quenching.

So sleep now in your

Liquid love,

And find me when you're

Thirsty.

Past Life Acquaintance

Can you feel me?

Do you feel me now?

It's been lifetimes but I

Swear that you are the only heart

I've ever known.

I knew you as soon as

I swallowed your

Vibration, and

Still I know you now.

I know everything I've never touched,

All the skin which has

Not yet met mine,

Each fingertip which has not yet

Explored my flesh.

I know it all,

And it makes more sense to me than

Most things, because

You are my oldest memory, and

My conception of reality is

Molded in your image.

So tell me that you can

Feel me now, and

Tell me that you

Remember.

Eternal Coupling

They say that

Change is the only

Constant, but

I'd argue that

Equally unwavering

Is love.

Forever and ever:

Love

And change,

Change,

And love.

I see no coincidence in their

Eternal coupling.

The Silence is Fine with Me

I will never expect you

To fill the empty space.

Silence is our right,

And everything else

Is a privilege.

Martyrdom

Buying a whole coffee

And only drinking half, I

Can only sip from the

Common cup anymore, I'm

Soaking in a sunset,

Steeping as long as the

Colors remain, but

Still I'm staying when they've

Faded and gone, this is

Fever rest,

Dreams laced with

Lambs and goldfinches, Lord

Take my body and

Deliver me, for

The serpent is

Coiled around my neck, and

This earthly desire is

Choking out my

Holy whispers.

September

I was born to a sacred grove

On a blood orange morning,

Swallowing the seeds of its glory,

Legs aching from the journey

Of a past life.

A day not as long as it

Could have been,

I washed them down with sips from

A sapphire sky.

Kaleidoscope world, this is

Prismatic déjà vu in

Shades of gold,

Another autumn dawn that

I have before

Awakened to.

Who am I?

I am a thousand best days ever,

The deafness that comes from both sound and silence,

All the songs you've never heard of,

Poems that speak of an infinite yesterday.

I am golden hours and blue dawns,

Naïveté and best intentions,

Hula hoops and honeybees,

Unfinished to-do lists.

I am every lost sweater and a watch never worn,

Mountain peaks and river beds,

Open windows and feet on the dashboard,

The shadows on the wall and their corresponding forms.

I am the willow in the breeze,

Sparkling water and hand-me-down jeans,

A cup of tea gone cold, and

Dirty dishes in the sink.

I am yesterday's tomorrow and

Tomorrow's yesterday.

I am not

What you seek;

I am

What you are.

You Can't Wake a Person Who is Pretending to be Asleep

Shut the sheep in their pasture, yes,

Shut them in before they wander out and

Taint my flowered meadow.

Usher them through the grimy tunnels of the

Underworld, endlessly traveling in

Crooked circles,

Checking boxes on

Blank sheets of paper.

Let them stamp their ashen footsteps in

The city dust,

The shape and pattern always

The same.

I'm taking off my shoes.

Inimitable

You cannot reuse

My nicknames.

My reputation

Will always

Precede them.

Ephemeral

I am both a time stamp on eternity and

A whisper in the wind.

Nothing to remember

Or forget.

Citrus Mother

Pomelo girl,

Carpels numbering seven,

A rare breed more

Skin than flesh,

That from which all others

Are sweeter hybrids.

Ritual

I remember us

Laughing

Shadow dancing in the pink light,

All skin and hair.

And suddenly the planets stopped dead

To revolve around us instead,

Because who could resist our gravity?

All bare feet and breath,

Writhing bodies warm and brown,

Hard and soft all at once,

Calloused hands and virgin thighs,

We were twice reborn,

Initiated as the sky surrendered blue,

Made gods by the light

Of a strawberry moon.

Was it Ever Really Here at All?

The sunset is and

Suddenly,

Is not.

Beauty is so often

The most fleeting

Illusion.

What Distinguishes a Word from a Sound?

Day after day, there was the lying.
Quiet lying,
The lying which can ease a temporary pain.
The lying which can never be forever.

In beds not my own and
On floors scattered with
Charming disarray,
In glistening fields and
From the lips of lovers too delicate
For an honest breath.

It was always the lying.

In rain and snow and
Unwelcome sunshine and
On eggshells long crushed under
Careless feet,
With scraps discarded and
In cryptic messages never delivered
By hand.

It was always the lying.

You Should Have Read the Warning Label

You left your cigarette

Out in the rain,

Still burning

Like you left me

Waiting

For you to hold me to your lips,

Abandoned and

Soaked to the bone, but

Still burning.

Now your mouth will

Taste like me, and

I will surely be

Slowly smothered.

Force of Nature

I stood atop a boulder

Atop my metaphoric world,

Slowly hypnotized by the swirl of the

Icy blue froth.

And it was then that I knew

What a compliment it was

To be called a

Force of nature.

Advaita

Duality is a

Delicate illusion,

Paradoxical in that

The interaction of two opposites

Can only ever create

A whole and perfect

Equilibrium.

From two

Comes one.

And from one

Comes everything.

It's Out of My Hands

Like a handful of water —

Always slipping

Through the cracks.

She's Dripping Down Your Chin

She came from the

Grove of empathy,

Plucked ripe from

Fruitful branches.

Oblivion

Walk with me, brave one,

Through afternoon machinery and

The mystery of night.

Predictable noon has

Never deceived me, but

Beyond dusk blue there is

No certainty.

Sweet danger,

I adore you, so

Should we never see

The morning, I

Won't cry.

Seventh Morning

The world is singing and
Sighing with relief.
There has not been a day like this
Since summer came to drape itself
Over every surface like
A hot blanket —
That which becomes in the night and
The peak of day a weapon
Of suffocation.
And now the earth,
Damp with September rain and
Chilled by the cool breath of this
Seventh morning,
Has shaken off its
Blistering confines.
So here I sit in the midst of this
Seasonal coronation,
No longer recoiling upon his touch,
Autumn sun,
King of all that is green and good and
Master of our
Human fate.
Autumn, let me breathe life into you,
Everything I have to give, and

Let it be enough to

Persuade you, to

Show you that we need you here with

Your calm and golden dawns, your

Spiraling decay into

Infallible renewal, autumn,

You are the catalyst of both

Life and death, and thus

You see that without you, we

Cannot die, and so

We beg to perish now,

With you, autumn,

So that we may rest our bones in

Winter white and

Come alive again in

Spring.

Show us, autumn, what it means to

Shed these layers.

And when the darkness lingers come October,

We will not be afraid, because

By your hand we have

Become light.

Distance

I think about you
Too small in a bed that fit the both of us
Perfectly, and
Your hands are folded on your chest now
Hollow, no
I'm never
Coming back.

I think about you
Estranged from me —
7 miles and 17 minutes
Of breath breathed by
Neither of us, and
I wonder who is
Sharing it in
The space between us where
We are not.

I think about you
Driving too fast with your left hand,
Spilling secrets in an empty car, and
Spitting them out the
Window, no
I'm never
Coming back.

Help, I Broke the Wall

Where does it go when it's

Gone?

Where can I find it in

The morning when I'm

Breathing again?

Stomping and

Soiling shallows, I am

Gasping and

Waiting

For the fuse to spark

My mind and bind

My lungs to

Bated breath.

Self-Inflicted

The only hell is

Expectation —

The assumption

Of doom is

Doom itself.

What Do I Really Have to Show but This Flesh?

I cannot tell you all I've seen,

Or all that I have been,

For now I know that I am just

A whisper in the wind.

No shape to bind or mold or break,

No form to move through space.

No hour hand decides my fate,

No time but present place.

Raised by the Internet

I want to love the

Internet, yes

I would say that I do,

Except

It can be oppressive

In the sense that

Everyone is looking for a

Remedy

Or an

Answer in the form of

Two seconds, eyes on the

Loading bar and it's

Never quick enough, so

You can never really have

Enough, you see it's

Hours scrolling for an

Answer

Or a

Remedy, let me tell you now that

Google

Doesn't have it.

Karmic Cycles

They say the well of

Psychic pains is

Bottomless, so

How many times

Will we bandage

The same wounds?

This rope and this pail

Are so worn and

So tired.

Moments of Full Being

I am.

I am standing alone in the kitchen

I am eating many small handfuls of dates

I am savoring the smoothness of my shaven thigh

I am.

I am.

I am casting my figure in mattress foam

I am longing for nothing and no one in particular

I am gathering a limb bouquet

I am.

I am.

I am hanging my head out the window

I am becoming the night air swallowed

I am severing inky inertia

I am.

Nature and Nurture are Not in Opposition

I know you are a woman.

You smell of nature and

Nurture and

Everything it takes

To mold a life

With your heart and

With your hands,

From womb to fingertips,

All soft and

Seeping into everything,

Light is born from you,

Woman.

Day after day and

Forever,

Light is born from you

And dies with you

Again and

Again.

You will never be

Invisible, because

You are all that the nothingness

Is not.

I know you are a woman.

The Wind Told Me You Were Leaving

Every word I speak to you is a brass-toned love song.

Some days I sing you ballads sad and slow and soft and
sweet.

Other days I am kicking up my heels and our tongues
are soon dancing to the tune of my sultry staccato.

I'm sorry it was a still evening the day you hung your
wind chime from the willow.

I'm sorry you never heard its quiescent clanging.

I sat under green tentacles those days after you left and I
learned its metallic song.

When you were gone I swear it crooned until the night
softened black to grey to glacier blue and picked up
warbling on at first light.

Now when I sing to you in unassuming conversation I
harmonize with lingering reverberations, and I trace the
ringing pitch of lonely hours, the echoes of your absence,
with my voice.

I'm sorry the breeze stayed shy and sleepy the day you
hung your wind chime from the willow.

You left in the morning and I swear those swaying limbs
could not feign silence in that steady shower of silver
sound.

Marinating there I plucked strands of sonic
incandescence and tucked them safely away between my
ribs.
I sing to you now and the willow whistles in time.
The willow whistles in time.

Diary of a Feeler

Maybe these pages don't

Love me like they used to.

Dump a gallon of blood here

Every few or so days,

Crisping edges with

Garnet desperation and

Scabbing over,

Staining and

Coagulating

Written hours.

You Saw the Ashes but Didn't Know I Was a Phoenix

You told me I was

Fragile; you were

Wrong.

We're Always Doing Both

I can't tell

If all this feeling

Is a side effect of

Living or

Dying.